YOU CHOOSE
BOOKS™

SO-AEE-114

WORLD WAR I

An Interactive History Adventure

by Gwenyth Swain

Consultant:
Timothy Solie
Adjunct Professor
Department of History
Minnesota State University, Mankato

CAPSTONE PRESS
a capstone imprint

You Choose Books are published by Capstone Press,
1710 Roe Crest Drive, North Mankato, Minnesota 56003.
www.capstonepub.com

Copyright © 2012 by Capstone Press, a Capstone imprint.
All rights reserved. No part of this publication may be reproduced in whole or in part,
or stored in a retrieval system, or transmitted in any form or by any means, electronic,
mechanical, photocopying, recording, or otherwise, without written permission of the
publisher. For information regarding permission, write to Capstone Press, 1710 Roe Crest Drive,
North Mankato, Minnesota 56003.

Books published by Capstone Press are manufactured with paper
containing at least 10 percent post-consumer waste.

Library of Congress Cataloging-in-Publication Data
Swain, Gwenyth, 1961–
  World War I: an interactive history adventure / by Gwenyth Swain.
    p. cm. —(You choose: history)
  Includes bibliographical references and index.
  ISBN 978-1-4296-6020-4 (library binding)
  ISBN 978-1-4296-7997-8 (paperback)
  1. World War, 1914–1918—Juvenile literature. I. Title. II. Title: World War One.
  D522.7.S95 2012
  940.3—dc23   2011033624

Editorial Credits
Catherine Neitge, managing editor; Bobbie Nuytten, designer; Wanda Winch, media researcher;
    Laura Manthe, production specialist

Photo Credits
Alamy: Classic Image, 55, Pictorial Press Ltd: 40, Rex/*Daily Mail*, 89; Bridgeman Art Library:
Roger-Viollet, Paris/Musée Franco-Americaine, Blerancourt, Chauny, France/Victor White,
77; Corbis: 45, 69, 79, Bettmann, 10, 26, 31, Hulton-Deutsch Collection, 72, 74, 81, Lebrecht
Music & Arts, 103, Lebrecht Music & Arts/Derek Bayes Aspect, 91, Michael Nicholson, 38;
Getty Images: Hulton Archive, cover, Pictorial Parade, 104, Topical Press Agency/A.R. Coster,
100; Library of Congress, Prints and Photograph Division, 24, 42, 57, 85; Mary Evans Picture
Library, 12, *Illustrated London News*, 18; National Archives and Record Administration
(NARA), 14–15, 49, 59, 62, 94; Newscom: akg-images, 22, Mirrorpix, 66; Superstock:
De Agostini, 6, Pantheon, 33, Everett Collection, 97

Printed in the United States of America in North Mankato, Minnesota.
022012   006609

TABLE OF CONTENTS

ABOUT YOUR ADVENTURE

YOU are a young person coming of age as the world explodes in war. What will you do? How will you face the horrors of a worldwide conflict?

In this book you'll explore how the choices people made meant the difference between life and death. The events you'll experience happened to real people.

Chapter One sets the scene. Then you choose which path to read. Follow the directions at the bottom of each page. The choices you make will change your outcome. After you finish one path, go back and read the others for new perspectives and more adventures.

*YOU CHOOSE the path
you take through history.*

Franz Ferdinand and his wife, Sophie, were shot and killed. He was heir to the throne of Austria-Hungary.

War in Europe!

It is the summer of 1914. War is brewing in Europe.

On June 28 Austria-Hungarian Archduke Franz Ferdinand and his wife, Sophie, are shot dead in the city of Sarajevo. Bosnian Serb Gavrilo Princip and several others are arrested for the crime. In July Austria-Hungary declares war on Serbia.

European countries quickly take sides. Germany and the Ottoman Empire join Austria-Hungary to form the Central Powers. France, Great Britain, and Russia form the Allied Powers.

Turn the page.

Most world leaders think the war will be over by Christmas. They are wrong. Dead wrong.

To protect their territory, soldiers across Europe dig trenches. From those trenches, they will fight a slow, deadly war. They will not only face the enemy. Soldiers will also struggle against bitter cold, summer heat, mud, rats, disease, and hunger.

From their trenches, soldiers go into battle. They wriggle through barbed wire, passing into the empty space of no man's land. This area lies between the Allied trenches and the Central Powers' trenches. They crawl on their stomachs as they try to capture enemy trenches. They dodge grenades and falling shells. They watch for signs of deadly poison gas.

Europe 1915

SWEDEN

North Sea

DENMARK

GREAT BRITAIN

NETHERLANDS

RUSSIA

London ⊗

Berlin ⊗

Somme R.

Passchendaele

BELGIUM

GERMANY

Amiens

Cantigny ●

R. Aisne

LUXEMBOURG

Belleau Wood

Paris ⊗

Verdun

Chateau-Thierry

Danube R.

Vienna ⊗

AUSTRIA-HUNGARY

Budapest ⊗

Marne R.

FRANCE

SWITZERLAND

ROMANIA

Allies
Central Powers
Neutral countries
Western Front

Bosnia

Belgrade ⊗

Sarajevo ●

SERBIA

ITALY

MONTENEGRO

BULGARIA

SPAIN

Mediterranean Sea

Rome ⊗

ALBANIA

0   150   300 mi.
0 150 300 km

9

The war hasn't yet touched you. That could change at any moment. Then you must decide how to react and how to survive.

→ To resist the Germans in Belgium, turn to page **11**.

→ To join the British military, turn to page **43**.

→ To join the war effort as an American, turn to page **75**.

Belgium's cavalry marched through Brussels at the beginning of the war.

CHAPTER 2

Belgium in Danger

"What does it mean?" your friend Elise asks. She's reading the newspaper headline: "Germany Demands Passage!"

"The Germans want to fight the French, and Belgium is in between," you answer.

"Belgium doesn't take sides. We're neutral, so we should be safe," Elise says, but she doesn't sound sure.

"Well, we can't spend time worrying," you say. "We need to fold these towels."

11

Turn the page.

You both get to work. It's early August 1914. A few weeks ago, you started nursing training at the Clinique, a hospital in Brussels, Belgium. You are excited, but you're tired. The head of nursing, Edith Cavell, is a British woman who believes in hard work.

"We can't be late getting these towels to Ward 3," you remind Elise. "Remember what happened when we were late to breakfast our first day here?"

Edith Cavell (seated) in 1915 with nurses she trained

"How could I forget? Matron Cavell made us work two extra hours washing bedpans!"

"Ugh!" you say, remembering the smell. "Nothing could be worse than that."

But you are wrong. Things could be much worse. The five biggest nations in Europe—France, Great Britain, Russia, Austria-Hungary, and Germany—will soon be at war. Your home in Belgium is caught in the middle.

The German army wants passage through Belgium to invade France. Germans say Belgians won't be hurt if they go along. But can they be trusted? During an invasion, will you be safer in the city or in the Belgian countryside? And if Germans occupy your country, will you go along or resist?

❖ To stay in Brussels and continue nurse training, turn to page **14**.

❖ To leave for the countryside, turn to page **17**.

German infantry on the battlefield in August 1914

On Tuesday, August 4, 1914, you wake early. Someone outside is yelling, "*Les Allemands!*" The Germans! You sink back into bed. Your country has just been invaded.

Elise rushes in. "We should have gone home," she wails.

"We're better off here," you say.

"But I'm scared," Elise says.

"So am I," you admit. "All we can do is work. That's what Matron Cavell says."

You admire the nurse in charge of training at the Clinique. She is so confident and fearless. Matron Cavell and the hosptial's founder, Dr. Antoine Depage, will treat everyone who comes to the Clinique. It doesn't matter if they are Belgian civilians or German soldiers.

Turn the page.

By August 20, Germans control Brussels. The British have joined the war on the French side, forming the Allies. Soon the Allies are retreating westward. As the Germans push toward France, many Allied soldiers are caught behind the lines.

"What if wounded Allied soldiers come here?" Elise whispers.

"I don't think the Germans will let us treat their enemies, even if we are a Red Cross hospital," you answer.

"So what should we do?" Elise asks.

"I could ask Dr. Depage's wife, Marie," you say. "Or maybe Matron Cavell will have advice."

➻ To talk with Madame Depage, turn to page **18**.

➻ To talk with Matron Cavell, turn to page **25**.

You want to be a nurse, but you worry about your brother, Stephan. He means well, but he gets into so much trouble.

By August 20, 1914, German soldiers occupy Brussels. The Belgian army fights back at Antwerp and Liege. But they are outnumbered. You decide at last to go home.

You join a flood of people leaving the city on foot. North of Brussels, you stop on a wooded hillside. You need to rest and eat. Suddenly you hear a voice.

"Help me … " A French soldier is hidden in the trees. His leg is bleeding from a cut from a sharp bayonet. "An accident," he tells you.

➤ *To refuse to help the soldier, turn to page 23.*

➤ *To help the soldier, turn to page 37.*

Antoine and Marie Depage
(seated) worked with nurses
to treat wounded soldiers.

When you speak to Madame Depage, she

asks you to go to the United States with her.

You're surprised, but flattered.

"But I don't want to leave," you say.

"Nonsense. You want to help the Clinique, don't you?"

You nod.

"Then come with me," says Madame Depage. "We will raise money for the hospital. You speak English, so you can translate for me. Besides, the Germans may be gone by the time we return."

"Perhaps," you say. But the German soldiers outside don't look like they plan to leave soon.

The United States is not in this war. You know it's safer there than here. But will you miss helping sick people?

➤ To go to the United States, turn to page **20**.

➤ To stay at the Clinique, turn to page **25**.

Friends of the Clinique help you and Madame Depage get to England. From there you sail to the United States. You help Madame Depage by speaking to large groups of Americans about donating money.

"We don't want war," a man says to you. "But we don't want Belgium to suffer. Let me write a check."

"Certainly," you say. "Merci!"

Nearly a year after Germany invaded Belgium, you and Madame Depage board the British ocean liner *Lusitania* for the trip home. Newspapers warn that German submarines are attacking ships on the Atlantic. But you have other things on your mind.

On the ship you meet a handsome American man, Joe Edwards. Like you, he wants to help sick and wounded people.

"I'm going to drive an ambulance for the French army," Joe says proudly. "You could visit me in Paris." You smile, but don't give him an answer.

On the afternoon of May 7, 1915, you're walking with Joe on the deck of the *Lusitania*. The ship is sailing near Ireland's coast.

Boom! A huge explosion rocks the ship. You and Joe are thrown to the deck.

"What's happening?" you shout.

"It must be a German torpedo," Joe yells back. Just then, another explosion tears the ship in two. "We're sinking!" he shouts. "Let's get to the lifeboats!"

Turn the page.

A single German torpedo doomed the *Lusitania*, which sank in 18 minutes.

Crew members are trying to lower lifeboats full of people into the water. But many of the boats accidentally dump people into the ocean.

"We're going to have to jump!" Joe shouts.

"No!" you scream, terrified.

➤ To jump with Joe, turn to page **33**.

➤ To stay on board, turn to page **35**.

"I can't help you here," you tell the injured soldier. "But go to Brussels. You'll find help there."

You give the man the Clinique's address. Then you continue until you reach your village. Your parents and Stephan are overjoyed to see you. The next day Stephan pulls you aside.

"I'm working for the Belgian resistance," he says. "You've got to help us. We're opening the dikes. The seawater will flood in—just as the Germans pass through. That should slow them down!"

Turn the page.

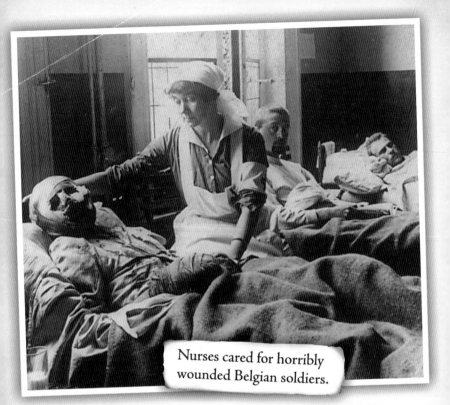

Nurses cared for horribly
wounded Belgian soldiers.

"Oh no, Stephan," you say. "We'll be killed if
the Germans catch us."

"Wouldn't you give your life for Belgium?"
he asks.

➤ *To help your brother, turn to page 39.*

➤ *To refuse, turn to page 41.*

You sit by the window in Matron Cavell's office. Below you see German soldiers across the street. "They will make our work harder," Matron says. "But we will do what must be done."

"How, Matron?"

"We will help everyone," she replies. "Especially wounded Belgian, French, and British soldiers. Then we will get them to Holland. There they will be safe."

"But what if the Germans find out, Matron? Won't we be sent to prison—or worse?"

"We will do what needs to be done," Matron repeats firmly. "And now, I need you to take out the trash."

You are placing the trash in the bin out back when someone comes up behind you.

"Who is it?" you ask, startled.

Turn the page.

Belgian soldiers helped a wounded comrade near Antwerp.

A man in a French army jacket stares at you. He is pale and breathing shallowly. You realize he is hurt.

"Come inside," you say.

"*Merci*," he whispers.

You lead the man down the narrow cellar steps.

"Stay here and be quiet," you say. "I must find help."

"Please be quick," he moans.

Before you reach Matron, you hear pounding at the front door. German voices are shouting.

The cellar is not a good hiding place. You will have to move the soldier—fast.

→ To take the soldier to the backyard, turn to page **28**.

→ To take the soldier upstairs, turn to page **30**.

"Hurry!" you whisper. "Germans are at the door!"

The French soldier is weak. You put his arm over your shoulder. Then the two of you go back up the cellar steps.

In the yard is a large wooden barrel. In the fall it will be filled with apples. Now it's almost empty.

"In there," you say. "Now!" You quickly grab an apple and replace the lid as a German soldier rushes into the yard.

"What are you doing?" he shouts in bad French.

➻ To stay silent, go to page 29.

➻ To talk to the German, turn to page 32.

The German soldier asks again, "What are you doing?" You shake your head and act like you don't understand as you munch on your apple. The soldier in the barrel keeps quiet.

After the Germans leave, you lift the lid and whisper, "Come out." You're so scared you can't believe that you can still speak. The soldier tells you his name is Louis.

With Matron Cavell's help, you clean Louis' wounds and put him into a hospital bed. You put a bandage around his jaw, even though he isn't hurt there.

"We can take it off when you eat," you say. "If you can't talk, no one will ask you questions. No one will guess you're not German." Louis nods.

➤ Turn to page 36.

The pounding at the door is louder. The Germans are here!

"Hurry," you tell the French soldier. "Do what I say, no matter what."

He follows you up the stairs to the hospital rooms. You remember an empty bed behind a large screen. The patients are sleeping. No one notices while you settle the soldier into bed. You grab bandages to wrap his head and shoulders.

Soon Germans are searching every inch of the Clinique. You stay by the soldier. When the Germans come close, you motion them away.

"Contagious!" you say. "Very contagious!"

Soldiers walked through the destruction in Ypres, Belgium.

Lucky for you, one of the Germans understands French. He tells the others to stay back. When the last German has left, you slide to the ground. You've saved the soldier, but you're so scared your knees won't hold you up anymore.

➤ *Turn to page 36.*

"I'm eating," you say. You show the German the apple.

He points at you and yells in German. You start trembling. What's worse, moans begin coming from the apple barrel.

The soldier grabs your wrists. Another German soldier rushes up and opens the barrel. The soldiers take you both away before Matron Cavell finds out what has happened. You are placed in St. Gilles Prison in Brussels. Months later the Germans find you guilty of helping the enemy. You are executed by a firing squad.

THE END

To follow another path, turn to page 9.
To read the conclusion, turn to page 101.

Passengers and crew struggled to get into *Lusitania* lifeboats.

You grab Joe's hand and take a deep breath. You both plunge into the Atlantic. As the shock of the cold water hits you, you swim to the surface, sputtering. Joe's head is also above water.

Turn the page.

"Look, there's a chair!" you say as you spot a wooden chair bobbing in the water. Both you and Joe grab it and hang on for dear life as you swim away from the wreckage. You're still clinging to the chair two hours later when a rescue boat arrives and scoops you to safety.

Later you are sad to learn that Madame Depage drowned in the sinking of the *Lusitania*, along with more than 1,000 others. You and Joe are two of the lucky 761 survivors. You both go to Paris. You work as a hospital nurse, and Joe drives an ambulance. The day the war ends, November 11, 1918, you and Joe are married in Paris. You look forward to a life of peace together.

34

THE END

To follow another path, turn to page 9.
To read the conclusion, turn to page 101.

"I can't!" you scream. Joe hesitates a second, and then jumps into the Atlantic without you. You watch him swim toward a lifeboat in the water and grab onto it.

You're just about to jump when a piece of metal from the ship slams into your head, knocking you unconscious. You slip quietly into the ocean, never to wake up.

THE END

To follow another path, turn to page 9.
To read the conclusion, turn to page 101.

You never thought you were brave. Now you've resisted the Germans!

Matron Cavell continues to treat Allied soldiers caught behind enemy lines. You help her in any way you can.

Nearly a year passes. On August 5, 1915, German police barge into the Clinique again. This time they arrest Matron Cavell. They put her in St. Gilles Prison. You visit whenever you can. You hope Matron will survive. But in October she is put on trial. A few days later, she is shot. You can't hide your tears, but you keep hiding Allied soldiers.

36

Unlike your teacher, you will survive this war. You will help rebuild your country after the fighting ends.

THE END

To follow another path, turn to page 9.
To read the conclusion, turn to page 101.

"You are lucky I'm a nurse," you tell the soldier. You dig in your bag for bandages and bind the man's wounds. Together you wait until dark.

The night sky is inky black, but you think you can find the next village. Someone there can help the soldier.

"Come," you whisper. "As long as we are quiet, we should be safe."

But you're wrong. You're inching down the road when a voice calls, "Halt!"

Both of you are captured by the Germans and put into a prison camp. The soldier is shot two weeks later, but you manage to stay alive.

Turn the page.

Soon after the war ends in 1918, you learn that your brother was killed in battle and Matron Cavell was executed in prison. There are too many bad memories in Belgium. You move to the United States to forget your sadness and start a new life.

A British card commemorated the shooting death of Edith Cavell.

THE END

To follow another path, turn to page 9.
To read the conclusion, turn to page 101.

"All right," you tell your brother. "I'll help you open the dikes. But it's only to be sure you don't get caught."

German troops advance during the night. They are making steady progress in their planned attack on France.

You live on flat farmland near the North Sea. You, Stephan, and the other resistance fighters blacken your faces and arms with boot polish. Then you sneak to the dikes. Together you open the floodgates holding back the sea. You know you've been successful when you hear distant shouts in German.

With your brother, you blend into the night. You walk around the floodwaters to get home.

Turn the page.

Barbed wire did not stop the German advance.

For the rest of the war, you and Stephan resist the Germans. You are lucky and are not caught. After peace comes, you go back to the Clinique to be a nurse. Your brother works on the family farm. You will be part of free Belgium's future.

THE END

To follow another path, turn to page 9.
To read the conclusion, turn to page 101.

"We can't do that. It's too dangerous," you tell your brother, but he turns and leaves.

Stephan and the others succeed in opening the floodgates. Their actions slow down the Germans. But many in the Belgian resistance are killed or put in prison.

When Stephan does not return, you find work in a hospital. You hope and pray he's safe.

You're happy in your work helping others. But the war and the occupation drag on. In 1918 a deadly illness called Spanish influenza arrives in Belgium. The hospital fills with patients. Soon you are sick. Just months before the war ends—and your brother returns home—you die of the flu.

THE END

To follow another path, turn to page 9.
To read the conclusion, turn to page 101.

Forward to Victory

ENLIST NOW

CHAPTER 3

Great Britain Joins the Fight

"Whoa!" you say to your horse, Nugget, as you stop your wagon. It is August 5, 1914. You've come to your small town in Wales to buy supplies. The streets are packed.

You knew the German army was crossing Belgium to invade France. But has something more happened? You jump down and give Nugget some water.

"What's going on?" you ask your friend David, who is a clerk at the grocer's shop.

Turn the page.

"War, that's what," he answers. "The Germans won't stay out of Belgium. The Belgians are fighting back. Great Britain declared war on Germany last night. I'm joining the army."

"But you're only 16!"

"Mother hates the Germans so much she'll lie about my age. Bet your parents would too."

Up until now you haven't thought much about war. Your cousin is in the cavalry. He rides a horse and carries a sword. Going to war like that wouldn't be bad. "How long do they figure this war will last?" you ask.

"We'll beat the Germans and be home for Christmas."

You want to give it more thought, but David is excited.

British cavalry soldiers would serve as infantry as the war progressed.

"I'm packing my bag," he says, "and joining the infantry!"

"I might join the cavalry …" you begin.

"Cavalry!" David says. "They'll take too long getting themselves and their horses together. There won't be any Germans left to fight! I'm off tomorrow. Be at the church by sunrise if you're going with me."

➤ To join the infantry, turn to page **46**.

➤ To join the cavalry, turn to page **49**.

45

The next morning you say good-bye to your family. By afternoon you and David reach the Royal Welsh Fusiliers, a well-known army regiment.

"You're of age?" The officer looks at you and David.

"Says so on our papers," you answer.

"All right then," he says.

An officer shouts for all soldiers to stand in ranks. You try to hold your gun like you know what you're doing. The officer calls for volunteers to go to France.

David steps forward. He wants you to follow.

"But we haven't even learned to fire a gun!" you whisper.

"We will soon," David replies.

➤ To stay in Wales for training, go to page **47**.

➤ To go immediately to France, turn to page **61**.

Training in Wales goes quickly. You miss David but make new friends.

You hear news of fierce battles. When you arrive in France in October, neither side is moving. Everyone is digging instead. Someone hands you a shovel.

"It's a barrier to stay behind. From here we can shoot the Boche," an old soldier says, using a slang word for Germans.

Allied and German trenches will soon reach from northern Belgium and France all the way to Switzerland. They will mark the Western Front, the line between enemy forces.

Turn the page.

At first your trench is chest-high. Then you dig deeper. You don't realize you are digging your home. You sleep on a shelf of dirt covered with straw. When it rains, your boots are caked in mud. It's hard to stay dry and impossible to stay warm. Rats steal your food. Lice make you itchy.

Every so often you and the Germans trade shots. You fire across the empty area between the trenches called no man's land.

One day in December, an officer asks for a volunteer to carry messages from one trench to another.

↠ *To be a messenger, turn to page 60.*

↠ *To stay in your trench, turn to page 64.*

Even horses wore gas masks during World War I.

The next morning you meet David at the church. "Good-bye," you tell him. "It's the cavalry for me."

Turn the page.

You've always loved horses. In the cavalry you are given a beautiful chestnut horse named Prince. You learn to ride him in formation and use your sword.

When your regiment and horses sail for France, you are scared but excited. The crossing is rough and the horses snort with fright, showing the whites of their eyes. You comfort Prince and the others.

"You have a way with animals," Sergeant Jones says. "We need men for the veterinary unit. Can we count on you?"

➤ To stay in the cavalry, go to page **51**.

➤ To treat sick and injured horses, turn to page **56**.

"Thank you, sir," you say. "I love horses. But my heart is set on the cavalry."

"Stay with your battalion," Sergeant Jones says. "And good luck to you."

Weeks later when you ride into battle, you remember that good luck wish. "Good luck to you, Prince," you whisper. Your horse is nervous. At night the guns pound like thunder. Exploding bombs light up the sky. Days are no better. Rain turns the ground into mud. Prince struggles to plow through it.

On the battlefield you and your fellow cavalrymen try to ride in formation. But this war is not like what you expected. Explosions make your ears ring. The air fills with smoke.

Turn the page.

The Germans have long-range guns. They shoot before you are close enough to draw your sword. When you are finally close enough to use the small gun you also carry, you feel Prince falling. He has been shot out from under you.

With explosions all around, you don't dare move. You hide behind your dead horse. He needs to be buried, but that is impossible. When night falls, you run. Tripping, you fall into a hole. You land on something soft. It's the dead body of another cavalryman. It is so dark and you are confused. Where can you go to be safe?

→ To keep running, go to page 53.

→ To stay in the hole, turn to page 72.

You leave the hole and run. On the dark battlefield, you can't tell which soldiers are German and which are British. Suddenly you run into a soldier on the ground. He says something like "ouch," but you're sure he's German. There's a flash of light. He is holding wire cutters. You know that each side sends soldiers ahead of an attack to cut communication lines.

"Give me those!" You struggle for the wire cutters. The German pulls out a gun. You grab a heavy rock. Just as a bullet hits your leg, you hit the soldier in the head. He falls to the side. After wrapping your leg in his torn shirt, you limp away.

53

Traveling by night, you reach a British army regiment. "I'm with the cavalry," you say. "How can I get back to them?"

"No going back now," an officer says. "They're too far away."

Turn the page.

You tell about meeting the German with the wire cutters. The officer is impressed. "We need someone like you to serve with our signal corps."

Soon you are crawling on your belly above the trenches. Your job is to keep communication lines open. Officers rely on the wires. They use portable field telephones to pass messages in code. Before a battle you carry wire cutters and a gun. You cut paths through barbed wire and crawl through the empty space of no man's land.

Then you do just as the German did. You look for enemy wires to cut. It's a dangerous job.

One foggy day in no man's land, you see a huge metal machine moving near the French trenches. The machine crushes the ground underneath. It rolls over trenches and into no man's land. It's coming nearer. What should you do?

➤ To stay low, turn to page **70**.

➤ To run, turn to page **71**.

French soldiers wearing gas
masks laid telephone wire.

This is a chance to work full-time with the animals. "Yes, sir," you tell the sergeant.

By dawn you are leading horses off the boat. You help the cavalry saddle up and mount. You then help set up a horse hospital at a farm not far from the fighting. You don't wait long for patients. Tired, thin soldiers arrive from the front. They lead injured horses. Some have cut and bleeding legs from barbed wire. Others have hoof problems from standing in deep, wet mud. Still more have shrapnel wounds from flying bits of metal.

"You see the best of the lot," a soldier says. "The others we shoot on the spot. Less pain for them."

You nod. It's your job to help the veterinarians nurse the horses back to health. When horses begin to recover, you lead them around the farm. As soon as you can ride them, you send the horses back. It's hard to see them go.

The British, French, U.S., and German armies all had veterinary corps.

ARE YOU FOND OF HORSES

U.S. ARMY

The
VETERINARY CORPS

INSTRUCTS YOU IN THEIR CARE AND TREATMENT RIDING AND DRIVING

ALSO MEAT AND DAIRY INSPECTION ENLIST TO DAY.

SEE ARMY RECRUITING OFFICER AT

The war goes on, month after month, year after year. You treat hundreds of horses. Over time you see fewer horses. War is changing.

Turn the page.

Generals don't use cavalry as much. But in the muddy battlegrounds, where trucks get stuck, horses still pull large guns on carts. The horses you treat are often nearly starving and worn out. They are being starved to death. The soldiers who come with them look exhausted as well.

Death is all around. So you can hardly believe it when the war ends. On November 11, 1918, the Allies and the Germans sign an armistice. The Allies have won the war. You'll finally get to go home. You can't wait to see your family and your old horse, Nugget, again.

THE END

To follow another path, turn to page 9.
To read the conclusion, turn to page 101.

An American flag was hoisted near Etraye, France, on November 11, 1918, the day the war ended.

"I'll go, sir," you say.

"Good," says the officer. "Take these messages to the command post at the next trench. You'll have to go above ground for a short while."

You tuck the messages into your uniform. Carefully you climb out of the trench. Luck is with you. No one fires. You deliver your messages.

You head back as night falls. You count on darkness to keep you safe. But you don't count on not being able to see what is in front of you. You stumble over a large rock, making noise.

From a German lookout post, someone takes a lucky shot. You fall to your knees on the cold, hard ground. News of your death reaches your family in Wales just before Christmas.

THE END

To follow another path, turn to page 9.
To read the conclusion, turn to page 101.

Once you reach France, you head for the fighting. French people cheer as you march through cities and towns. You stop only at night, camping on the ground. Your goal is the French-Belgian border. There you will join British, French, and Belgian troops, called the Allies. All is calm until you reach the village of Le Cateau-Cambrésis.

"Finally," you say. "Some of our troops are here."

"But they're not marching toward Belgium," David replies.

He's right. The Allies are on the run. They are turning away from the Germans. Soon the call comes to dig in and fight.

Turn the page.

You crouch behind a rock ledge. Fortunately the older soldiers taught you how to use your rifle. Now you aim toward the woods. Crack!

German soldiers fired from their well-protected trenches.

Gunshots are followed by mortar shells. The hillside seems to explode. The heavy cloud of smoke makes it hard to know where to shoot.

Pfut! An explosion shakes you. You see David lying nearby. Blood is gushing from a wound to his head. You rush to his side but forget to stay low to the ground. A German bullet strikes you, and you fall. You barely realize what has happened. A few minutes later, both you and David are dead on the ground.

THE END

To follow another path, turn to page 9.
To read the conclusion, turn to page 101.

The soldier in the trench next to yours volunteers to deliver the messages. When he doesn't come back, you're sad but relieved that you stayed in your trench.

By December 24 you are tired and homesick. You miss your family members, who are celebrating the Christmas holiday. Maybe the Germans feel the same way. You grab a board and write a quick message: "Happy Christmas!"

You raise the board above the trench. Instead of firing, you hear happy shouting.

An old soldier starts singing Christmas songs. In the German trench, others sing "Stille Nacht," the German "Silent Night."

Before long a British soldier walks out into no man's land. He offers a packet of cookies and a can of beef soup to the Germans. The Germans come up from their trenches. They have more food to share.

"Is it a trap?" you ask John, the soldier next to you.

"Could be. I'm not going over there."

More than anything you want Christmas to be a day of peace. You're afraid, but take the risk. You pick your way over barbed wire, joining German and British soldiers.

The Christmas party lasts most of the day. You show a German soldier a photograph of your parents in Wales. He shows you a picture of his girlfriend. "She's pretty," you say, hoping he understands.

Turn the page.

German and British soldiers enjoyed their temporary Christmas truce.

Not a single shot is fired. There are no presents that Christmas, but the brief truce is the best gift of all.

A short time later mortar rounds blast deep holes near your trench. The war is back in full swing. Your battalion moves to Ypres, near the French border, in April. Suddenly one morning a lookout yells, "Gas!"

Germans have used tear gas before. So have the French. It smells like onions and makes you cry. Something tells you this gas is different.

A greenish-yellow cloud spreads over the trench. You run, trying to keep ahead of it. Soldiers are coughing and screaming. One is rubbing his eyes. "I can't see!" he yells.

Turn the page.

This is one of the first uses of poison chlorine gas in war. Within seconds of breathing the gas soldiers start to choke. It's horrible! You don't know what to do. You have a terrible feeling that this isn't the only time deadly gas will be used. You expect it will serve as a mighty weapon until the war is finally over.

You run and keep running until you're away from the gas. You manage to reach safety, but your lungs have been damaged. For the rest of your life, you will suffer the effects of the poison gas.

THE END

To follow another path, turn to page 9.
To read the conclusion, turn to page 101.

Soldiers ran through a
cloud of toxic gas.

You panic for a moment. Then you remember that the French car company Renault is making a metal vehicle called a tank. It is meant to be attack-proof. This tank is designed to go over trenches and smash the barbed wire of no man's land.

You cheer and move forward, still crouched low. With tanks and other new weapons, you are hopeful. This war has been long and hard, but you believe you are on the winning side. You hope with all your heart that you'll survive.

THE END

To follow another path, turn to page 9.
To read the conclusion, turn to page 101.

Fear grips you. Will you be crushed under the giant machine? Even though you are disobeying orders, you run.

"Get down!" another soldier shouts.

You're too afraid to stop. You keep running.

"It's a French tank! It's on our side!" the soldier yells.

"What … ?" Your words are cut short. You've been shot. For hours you lie on the battlefield, wounded. At last two medics find you. They take you first to a battlefield clinic, then to an ambulance. But it's too late. Your wounds are too serious. You and many others never come home.

THE END

To follow another path, turn to page 9.
To read the conclusion, turn to page 101.

You think over your options. If you run, you may be shot. The hole is safe for now. You move as far away as you can from the dead soldier's body.

The fighting gets worse as the night goes on. Shells fall close by and explode. The sound deafens you. Explosions continue all night.

British soldiers wearing gas masks fired a machine gun from their trench.

When you are found, you are shaking. Your ears are ringing. You stare off into space. You cannot speak. Even though you are not bleeding or wounded, you are sent to an army hospital.

"Shell shock," a doctor says, looking you over. "It's new. We have more cases every day. You men see such horrible things. At some point, you crack."

You nod. The doctor's words make sense.

The doctor sends you to a hospital in England, where you slowly recover. Lightning makes you jump. Loud noises cause you to scream in pain. By November 1918, when the war finally ends, you are well enough to go home. But like thousands of your fellow soldiers, you will never be the same.

THE END

To follow another path, turn to page 9.
To read the conclusion, turn to page 101.

Allied soldiers waited in their trenches for a battle to begin.

CHAPTER 4

Americans Heed the Call

It's spring 1915. You're a student at Syracuse University in New York. You dream of adventure, but your parents want you to be a doctor.

"You can help people as a doctor," Dad says. "Who could you help as an adventurer?"

Up to now, you haven't had an answer. But Europe is in the middle of a great war. You've heard about something called the AFS.

"It stands for American Field Service," your friend Al says. "You drive an ambulance. You take the wounded from the front to hospitals in France."

Turn the page.

"What an adventure!" you say. "What do I have to do to join?"

"That's the hard part," says Al. "You have to pay your way to France. Then you have to pay for food and a bed."

"So it's all volunteers?"

"Yep. Volunteers who can drive and speak French. You took French in high school and college, didn't you?"

"Yes," you say. "I wonder if my parents will be upset if I go."

→ To join the American Field Service, go to page 77.

→ To stay in school, turn to page 83.

American Field Service volunteers participated in every major French battle.

"When do you leave?" Al asks.

"Tomorrow," you answer. You can hardly believe it. Dad wasn't hard to convince. "You can finish medical school after the war," he told you. "This will be good training."

Turn the page.

"Wish I could go," Al says. "My parents support this war, but they think school's more important now."

When you get to the American Hospital in Paris, you begin training to be an ambulance driver. Your work isn't easy. Everyone refers to the Model Ts as cars, although they are more like trucks. You've never driven a car before. Most kids your age haven't. Cars are still fairly rare and expensive. Your teacher, Henri du Charme, explains how to use the hand crank to start the engine when it's cold. He shows you how to change the tires. You wish cranks and tires were more exciting.

Ambulances transported the wounded to field hospitals.

Next Henri takes you to the back of the car and explains the layout. "The bed of the car is longer than normal," he explains. "That way injured solders can lie on stretchers on the floor inside."

Turn the page.

You climb up under the canvas top. At your waist are spaces for more stretchers.

A man runs out of the office. "We need drivers now!" he shouts. "The French need us on the front. There are so many wounded. Who's trained and ready to go?"

Henri looks at you. He leaves it to you to decide if you're ready.

➤ *To go to the front, go to page* **81**.

➤ *To continue your training, turn to page* **86**.

Stretcher bearers carried a wounded comrade through the mud.

You're still not sure how to put your car in reverse, but you set off to the front. An ambulance can go up to 55 miles per hour, but you never push the engine past 30. Before long you hear booms and crashes. You're getting close to the battle.

Turn the page.

First you check in at the field hospital. This is where you will take the wounded. An American doctor tells you to go to the *poste de secours*. That means "place of help" in English. It's the name used for small emergency hospitals just behind the front lines.

The roads get worse near the front. At the *poste* another car has just taken away a load of soldiers. But the doctor tells you more wounded will be coming in soon.

"Help us!" A medic shoves the handles of a stretcher toward you. You're supposed to stay with your ambulance, but it's clear that the medics need help.

➼ *To go with the medic into battle, turn to page* **88**.

➼ *To stay with the ambulance, turn to page* **92**.

Your parents want you to stay home and finish your studies. You reluctantly agree. Soon it's 1917. The war continues, but the United States stays out of it.

That soon changes. In January British code breakers decode a telegram from German Foreign Minister Arthur Zimmermann to the German ambassador to Mexico. In the telegram Zimmermann outlines a plan to get Mexico to join Germany in a war against the United States. American newspapers publish the telegram in March.

On April 6, 1917, the U.S. Congress declares war on Germany. Soon your college friends are signing up to fight overseas. But your parents insist you stay in school. Finally you graduate in 1918.

Turn the page.

"Join the army with me," your friend and fellow graduate Frank says.

"I think I'd rather be a medic," you say.

"Come with me," Frank says. "You'll be right on the front lines in the infantry."

❧ To join the infantry, turn to page **96**.

❧ To be an army medic, turn to page **98**.

I WANT YOU FOR U.S.ARMY

NEAREST RECRUITING STATION

More than 4 million copies of the famous recruiting poster were printed in 1917 and 1918.

"I would go," you tell Henri, "but I might wreck the car."

"You may be right," he says. "Someone else can go this time."

Over the next few days, your driving improves. When the office again asks for a volunteer, you go.

The field hospital where you will take the wounded is only a few miles from the front. But you don't hear any battle noises.

"There's an informal truce going on right now," Dr. Flandreau tells you. "It's been quiet for days."

"I'll go to the front anyway," you say.

"You can go," he replies. "But it will be a waste of time."

You hurry to the front, but the doctor is right. No wounded soldiers are waiting at the poste de secours, the small emergency hospital.

You wait for weeks. To pass the time, you practice your French, play cards, and write letters home.

The weather is wet and miserable. The road outside the poste turns into mud. You hope your ambulance won't get stuck. Mostly, you hope you won't die of boredom.

Finally, the rain stops. You are standing in the road outside the small hospital when you hear a noise. It's like a big bee buzzing. Before you can ask what it is, a soldier screams, "Take cover!"

You need to go somewhere fast. Should you run forward into the poste or back to your ambulance?

➧ *To go to the poste, turn to page* **90.**

➧ *To go to your ambulance, turn to page* **93.**

You're following the medic when you almost stumble over a wounded soldier. He's lying above the trench in the mud. Blood oozes from a wound in his side. German bullets are whizzing around you, but it will only take a minute to rescue the soldier. "Stop!" you shout to the medic. You help him load the wounded soldier on the stretcher. You each lift one end of the stretcher and hurry back to the waiting ambulance.

You're almost to safety when you feel a sharp pain in your back. You drop your end of the stretcher and slump to the ground. "You've been shot!" the medic says. He leans over you as you struggle to breathe. As he tries to stop your bleeding, the world starts to turn fuzzy and gray.

Troops went over the top of a trench during a fierce battle.

As you close your eyes for the last time, you hope the medic has better luck saving the injured soldier.

THE END

To follow another path, turn to page 9.
To read the conclusion, turn to page 101.

That buzzing noise reminds you of airplanes at an air show back home. But this is no show. The pilots are shooting from their planes.

You dive to the ground and start crawling toward the poste. You nearly make it, when pops and thuds surround you. A sick, warm feeling spreads through your gut. As you cough up blood, you realize that you've been shot.

The doctors try to save you, but fail. Your adventure in Europe ends almost before it began.

90

THE END

To follow another path, turn to page 9.
To read the conclusion, turn to page 101.

German biplanes had an iron cross or a black Greek cross emblem on their wings.

You're standing outside the ambulance when you hear a loud whizzing noise. You drop to the ground. When you get up, you see that a shell passed through the ambulance's canvas top. But otherwise the car is fine. It's a good thing you weren't inside! Soon medics come with wounded soldiers on stretchers. When the ambulance is full, you head to the field hospital.

The next day you are up early, tuning up your engine and making sure the ambulance is in good working order. With luck and hard work, you will have a great adventure and survive this terrible war.

THE END

To follow another path, turn to page 9.
To read the conclusion, turn to page 101.

You're closer to your ambulance than you are to the poste. You run to your car and jump in. Soon a battle starts in the sky between two small airplanes—one French and the other German. The pilots are shooting rounds of ammunition. Stray bullets strike the ground around you like deadly hailstones.

Suddenly the German flyer hits his mark. The French plane starts a nosedive toward the ground. It's coming straight for you!

"No!" you scream as you hide your eyes. You're sure the plane will hit you. But instead it lands on a barn a few yards away. You survived this attack, but a new battle is beginning.

"THUD! THUD! THUD!"

Turn the page.

Soldiers positioned a gun as they prepared for battle.

The ground shakes each time a grenade or shell lands. You see parts of a nearby trench crumbling. Soldiers shout for help, but you are trained to stay with your ambulance.

Stretchers soon arrive at the poste. Medics load the soldiers with the most serious injuries into your car. Once you have a full load, you step on the gas.

But the road is too muddy. The ambulance is stuck. You get out to push from behind. Just as you and the medics get the ambulance free of the mud, you feel your left shoulder being torn apart. You've been hit.

Somehow you drive one-handed and bleeding to the field hospital. But you can't go back to the front. Your wound is too serious. You need a very long time to heal. By the time you recover, the war is over. Your adventure in France was short but thrilling.

95

THE END

To follow another path, turn to page 9.
To read the conclusion, turn to page 101.

You and Frank travel by train to Camp Funston, Kansas. It opened just months after war was declared. You will train there for a few weeks before leaving for France. But after you've been there several days, you notice fewer soldiers showing up each morning.

"What's going on?" you ask Frank.

"I heard some officers saying a lot of guys are coming down with the Spanish flu," says Frank. "Some were even sick when they got here. It's bad—people are dying from it."

"We're strong," you tell Frank. "We won't get sick." But a few days later, you wake up with aching muscles and a high fever.

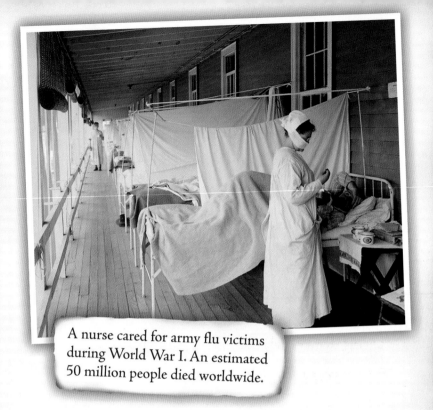

A nurse cared for army flu victims during World War I. An estimated 50 million people died worldwide.

Frank takes you to the camp's makeshift hospital, but the doctors there can't do anything for you. You're one of many young soldiers who die before reaching the battlefields of France.

THE END

To follow another path, turn to page 9.
To read the conclusion, turn to page 101.

It's the end of your first day at the new field hospital. You've already lost track of how many wounded men you've treated. There are injuries from hand grenades thrown by the enemy. You see lots of shrapnel, which are bits of metal from exploding shells or mines. Some of the wounded were too close to mortar shells. They've lost arms or legs. Other soldiers couldn't escape poison gas. Now their eyes and lungs are damaged. You wish you could do more than just treat their pain.

Early one morning an ambulance pulls up. The driver honks the horn. You run down to meet the wounded. The driver calls out a greeting to you in French. "*Bonjour!*"

It takes you a minute to recognize your college buddy Al.

"How are you, pal?" you ask.

"Just swell," he answers. He's dirty, thin, and needs a shave. But underneath, he's the same old Al. Looks as if he found a way to join the AFS after all.

You and Al see each other from time to time over the next year and a half. After the fighting ends in November 1918, you share a ride on the ship taking you both safely home.

THE END

To follow another path, turn to page 9.
To read the conclusion, turn to page 101.

An American soldier shook hands with a child as troops marched through London.

CHAPTER 5

The Great War

During World War I, from 1914 to 1918, soldiers fought not just in France and Belgium, but across most of Europe. They also fought on the Suez Canal and elsewhere in Egypt, as well as in Iraq and Bulgaria. Before the war no one had seen fighting on such a worldwide scale.

It wasn't just size that made World War I different. The conflict was a turning point in warfare. Everything from uniforms to tactics to weapons changed.

Turn the page.

French soldiers went to war in 1914 wearing bright red pants and cloth hats. By 1918 uniform colors blended into the landscape. Metal helmets protected soldiers' heads.

In 1914 British cavalry rode into battle in formation and carried long swords. Leaders soon decided that swords would not win a modern war.

New tactics played a big role. Poison gas sent over the lines damaged soldiers' lungs. Soon soldiers carried gas masks in their packs.

For the first time in a major war, small airplanes flew overhead. Pilots gathered information. Sometimes they used their guns to target troops on the ground or enemy aircraft.

Newly invented tanks cleared the way across dangerous battlefields and over the tops of deep trenches. Their armor protected the soldiers inside from enemy fire.

At first small planes flew reconnaissance missions but then added guns.

In the summer of 1914, most soldiers went to war thinking that they would be home for Christmas. They were sure that the war would be short. They thought all the battles would be decisive, with a clear winner and loser. None of these things happened.

World War I was called
The Great War.

Slowed down by Belgian resistance and by Allied troops, the Germans could not carry out their plan to capture Paris. By fall 1914 armies were digging trenches near the French-Belgian border. They would move little over the next few years. As hard as soldiers fought, the forces were evenly matched. With the arrival of U.S. troops in 1917, the Allies finally gained the advantage.

On November 11, 1918, an armistice was signed. More than 8.5 million soldiers had died in the slaughter. Even more civilians lost their lives. Soldiers could finally go home. Civilians could pick up the pieces of their lives.

Peace in Europe, however, did not last long. Germany suffered economically and bitter feelings grew. Those who fought in the conflict called it "the war to end all wars." But World War I did not bring an end to war. By 1939 Europe was a battlefield once more.

Timeline

June 28, 1914—Archduke Franz Ferdinand, heir to the throne in Austria-Hungary, is shot dead in Sarajevo, Bosnia, by Serbian Gavrilo Princip.

July 28, 1914—Austria-Hungary declares war on Serbia.

August 1, 1914—Germany declares war on Russia.

August 3, 1914—Germany declares war on France.

August 4, 1914—Germany invades Belgium; Great Britain declares war on Germany.

August 20, 1914—German troops occupy the city of Brussels, Belgium.

December 1914—For several days around Christmas, German and Allied troops make an unofficial truce along the front lines in Europe.

April 1915—American volunteers start driving ambulances to the front lines to carry away injured British and French soldiers.

April 22, 1915—Germans use chlorine gas during the Second Battle of Ypres.

May 7, 1915—A German submarine sinks the ocean liner *Lusitania*, killing 1,198 people.

August 5, 1915—British nurse Edith Cavell is jailed along with others suspected of resisting German authorities in Belgium; she is executed in October.

July 1, 1916—The Battle of the Somme begins in France; 58,000 British troops die the first day of the battle.

January 1917—German Foreign Minister Arthur Zimmermann sends a telegram to the German ambassador to Mexico suggesting that Germany join Mexico in war against the United States.

April 6, 1917—The United States declares war on Germany.

June 25, 1917—The first American troops arrive in France.

September 27, 1918—Allied troops break through German lines.

November 11, 1918—The Allied powers sign an armistice with Germany.

June 28, 1919—The Treaty of Versailles is signed in France; World War I is officially over.

OTHER PATHS TO EXPLORE

In this book you've seen how the events experienced during the war look different from three points of view.

Perspectives on history are as varied as the people who lived it. You can explore other paths on your own. Seeing history from many points of view is an important part of understanding it.

Here are ideas for other points of view to explore:

+ Throughout World War I, Americans stepped forward to send food aid to Belgium. Donations of grain helped Belgians avoid starvation. What would it have been like to be a volunteer with the Commission for Relief in Belgium?

+ World War I was the first conflict in which aircraft played an important role in warfare. What would it have been like to fly an airplane on an intelligence mission or take part in an aerial duel during the war?

+ Even before the United States declared war on Germany, many Americans of German descent felt hostility and distrust from other Americans. What would it have been like to be someone of German descent living in the United States during wartime?

READ MORE

Batten, Jack. *Silent in an Evil Time: The Brave War of Edith Cavell.* Plattsburgh, N.Y.: Tundra Books of Northern New York, 2007.

Morpurgo, Michael. *War Horse.* New York: Scholastic Press, 2007.

Murphy, Jim. *Truce: The Day the Soldiers Stopped Fighting.* New York: Scholastic Press, 2009.

INTERNET SITES

109

FactHound offers a safe, fun way to find Internet sites related to this book. All of the sites on FactHound have been researched by our staff.

Here's all you do:
Visit *www.facthound.com*
Type in this code: 9781429660204

GLOSSARY

armistice (ARM-iss-tiss)—a formal agreement to end the fighting during a war

infantry (IN-fuhn-tree)—soldiers trained to fight on foot

influenza (in-floo-EN-zuh)—a very contagious virus; a worldwide epidemic of a strain called Spanish influenza killed millions in 1918 and 1919

invasion (in-VAY-shuhn)—unwanted entry into someone's territory

neutral (NOO-truhl)—not taking sides

occupation (awk-yuh-PAY-shuhn)—the possession of a country in wartime by force

resistance (ri-ZISS-tuhnss)—a group of people in an occupied country who work in secret against the occupying power

shell shock (SHEL SHOK)—a condition where patients become mentally confused, upset, or exhausted after being in battle; now known as post-traumatic stress disorder

shrapnel (SHRAP-nuhl)—small pieces of metal that are scattered by an exploding shell or bomb

Western Front (WESS-turn FRUHNT)—the line of fighting and trenches in World War I stretching from the North Sea to the French-Swiss border

BIBLIOGRAPHY

Clowes, Peter. *"Edith Cavell: World War I Nurse and Heroine."* 12 June 2006. 2 Sept. 2011. www.historynet.com/edith-cavell-world-war-i-nurse-and-heroine.htm

Ellis, John. *Eye-Deep in Hell: Trench Warfare in World War I.* Baltimore: Johns Hopkins University Press, 1989.

Essen, Léon van der. *A Short History of Belgium: With a Special Chapter on "Belgium During the Great War."* Chicago: University of Chicago Press, 1920.

Hansen, Arlen J. *Gentlemen Volunteers: The Story of the American Ambulance Drivers in the Great War, August 1914–September 1918.* New York: Arcade Pub., 1996.

Howard, Michael. *The First World War: A Very Short Introduction.* New York: Oxford University Press, 2007.

Knight, Private Chris. *"Memoirs & Diaries—A Cavalry Brigade at Cambrai, November 1917."* 2 Sept. 2011. www.firstworldwar.com/diaries/cavalrybrigadeatcambrai.htm

Richards, Private Frank. *Old Soldiers Never Die.* London: Faber & Faber, 1933.

Seymour, James William Davenport, ed. *History of the American Field Service in France, "Friends of France," 1914–1917.* Boston: Houghton Mifflin Company, 1920.

Skaife, E. O. *A Short History of the Royal Welsh Fusiliers.* London: Gale & Polden, 1925.

Stone, Norman. *World War One: A Short History.* New York: Basic Books, 2009.

INDEX